More OF
My Recipes are for the Birds

by **Irene Cosgrove**
Illustrated by
Ed Cosgrove

DOUBLEDAY
New York London Toronto Sydney Auckland

Published by Doubleday, a division of Bantam Doubleday Dell
Publishing Group, Inc., 666 Fifth Avenue, New York, New York
10103.

Doubleday and the portrayal of an anchor with a dolphin are
trademarks of Doubleday, a division of Bantam Doubleday Dell
Publishing Group, Inc.

Library of Congress Cataloging-in-Publication Data

Cosgrove, Irene.
    More of my recipes are for the birds / Irene and Ed Cosgrove.—
1st ed.
        p.   cm.
    ISBN 0-385-26501-8
    1. Birds—Food. 2. Bird feeders. I. Cosgrove, Ed. II. Title.
QL676.5.C57   1989
639.9'78—dc19   89-30247
                                                                  CIP

Introduction

*Bird feeding will increase our interest
in nature and deepen our concern for
the environment. By setting up feeding
stations in our backyards, we begin
in a very small way, to be aware of
and to understand the science of ecology.
Whether permanent residents or winter
visitants, birds will be attracted to your
feeders if you keep them stocked.
The following gourmet recipes
will be enjoyed by all.*

The Secondary Feeding Station

Blackbirds, Grackles, Cowbirds, Starlings and Crows can be aggressive and quite pushy in the company of small birds. However, they are nervous and suspicious of humans and prefer not to be too close to the house or your main feeders. Set up a ground feeder and a plastic coated wire basket for suet and tidbits. The birds can be attracted to the feeder by scattering small pieces of white bread or cracked corn on the ground. These restless vagrants will drop in, have a snack, and before you know it, they are on their way.

About The Ingredients

Beef Suet
Beef suet is very important in providing energy and warmth during the cold winter months. In preparing suet, always put it through a meat grinder first. To render, melt the suet in a double boiler, cool, then reheat.

Sand
Grit is needed to grind and digest the coarse foods that birds eat. Ordinary beach sand will do, or you can provide commercial bird gravel.

Kitchen Scraps
Store your left over cake, donuts, cookies and pie crust in a plastic container with cover. Keep crusts and stale bread in another.

Seeds and Grains
Thistle, millet, sunflower seeds, cracked corn, peanut hearts and wild bird seed can be bought at your local feed shop.

BACKYARD BREAKFAST

2½ Cups rendered suet   1   Cup Raisin Bran
1   Cup Grapenuts   1   Cup Puffed Wheat
                          ½ Tsp. sand

Render the suet (see About The Ingredients). Put the Grapenuts, Raisin Bran and Puffed Wheat into an 8″ x 8″ pan and sprinkle with sand. Pour the rendered suet over dry ingredients. Refrigerate till firm. Cut into squares and place on feeder tray or ground.

CHEEP CHEEP CORNBREAD

1	Cup yellow cornmeal	4	Tsp. baking powder
½	Cup cracked corn	1	Cup milk
1	Ground eggshell	1	Egg, beaten
1	Cup flour	¼	Cup bacon drippings

Heat oven to 400°F. Combine dry ingredients. Add milk, egg and bacon drippings. Mix with spoon and pour into 8″ x 8″ pan. Bake 20-25 minutes. When cool, cut into cubes and serve on feeder tray or ground.

The Red-winged Blackbird is one of the first birds to arrive in the spring. This early bird consumes huge quantities of insects and weed seeds.

BLACKBIRD BISCUITS

2⅓ Cups biscuit mix   ⅔ Cup cold water
½   Cup white proso millet

Mix all ingredients till dough forms, then beat for 30 seconds. Drop by spoonfuls onto ungreased cookie sheet. Bake at 450° for 8 to 10 minutes. These biscuits can be put into wire basket or scattered on ground at secondary feeding station.

The Indigo Bunting male is an overall deep blue. They are seen at feeding stations during spring and fall migrations.

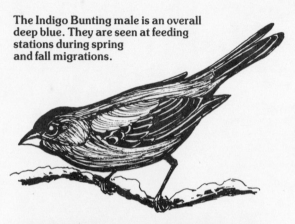

BUNTING BREAD

1 Cup rendered suet
4 Slices cracked wheat bread
½ Cup thistle seed

Pour rendered suet into a soup plate, stir in thistle seed and soak slices of cracked wheat bread in mixture. Refrigerate until hardened, cut and serve on low feeder tray.

The Gray Catbird arrives in our gardens in May and can be seen on the ground or in low bushes. Its call is a distinct cat-like mew.

CATBIRD CAKE

1	Cup raisins	1	Tbs. baking soda
1½	Cups water	1	Cup sugar
1	Heaping tbs. shortening	2	Cups flour

Simmer the raisins in the water for 20 minutes. Drain and reserve 1 cup liquid. To the liquid, add the shortening and the baking soda and let stand to cool. Add 1 cup sugar, 2 cups flour and stir in raisins. Pour into an 8″ x 8″ pan and bake at 375° for 1 hour. Serve in pieces at ground feeder.

Brown-headed Cowbirds traveling in mixed flocks will sporadically visit your feeding station. They have a habit of laying their eggs in other birds' nests.

COWBIRD COOKIES

1 Cup (2 sticks) margarine
¼ Cup sugar

2 Cups flour
White proso millet

In a bowl, cream margarine and sugar. Add the flour and mix well. Shape rounded tablespoonfuls of dough into balls; roll in white proso millet, and place on ungreased cookie sheet. Bake at 400°F. for 10 to 12 minutes. Serve on ground or in wire basket at secondary feeding station.

The Brown Creeper,
with its curved bill,
will always fly to the base of
a tree and climb it like a
spiral staircase in search
of insects and larvae.

CREEPER CREAMY SPREAD

½ Cup rendered suet
1   Cup creamy peanut butter

Combine one cup of creamy peanut butter with the rendered suet and mix thoroughly. Spread on tree trunks.

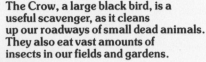

The Crow, a large black bird, is a useful scavenger, as it cleans up our roadways of small dead animals. They also eat vast amounts of insects in our fields and gardens.

CROW CANAPÉS

1   Cup rendered suet
Table scraps, including meat

1   Slice white bread
½ Cup cracked corn

Put table scraps into an 8″ x 8″ pan. Add slice of bread, in pieces and cracked corn. Pour the rendered suet over all ingredients and allow to harden in refrigerator. Cut into pieces and serve in plastic wired feeder or on the ground at the secondary station.

The Common Grackle is an iridescent, long tailed bird with yellow eyes. Crackles travel in mixed flocks and are infrequent visitors at your feeding station.

GRACKLE GRITS

1 Cup mashed potatoes	½ Cup cottage cheese
	1 Cup bakery scraps

Mix these three ingredients with a fork until you are able to shape into small balls. Toss on the ground at your secondary feeding station. You may substitute leftover rice for potatoes.

The Northern Oriole male is a bright orange and black bird. Orioles build deep pendant nests in large shade trees and although insect eaters, they can be enticed to your feeders with fruits and berries.

ORIOLE HORS D'OEUVRES

Oranges	Figs
Apples	Dried apricots
Bananas	Bread crumbs

During the summer months, the Northern Oriole will enjoy oranges, apples and bananas, split and served on a spiked fruit feeder—ah, hors d'oeuvres before a hearty meal of garden grubs! During the fall or early winter, try figs, cooked dried apricots and hard crusts of bread, spread with grape or apple.

The Pine Siskin, a seed eater, has pale brown streakings with yellow at the base of the tail and in the wings. Its bill is thinner than that of other finches.

SISKIN SUPREME

1 Cup rendered suet	1 Cup thistle seed
½ Cup bacon drippings	½ Cup peanut hearts

Combine the rendered suet with the bacon drippings and pour over the thistle seed and peanut hearts. Allow to cool and harden in refrigerator. Serve in netted hanging bags.

The Starling, in summer a short-tailed glossy-black bird with yellow bill, changes to a heavily speckled brown billed bird in winter. Starlings have voracious appetites and consume huge quantities of harmful insects and weed seeds.

STARLING SURPRISE

1 Cup rendered suet	½ Cup warm water
½ Cup dry dog food	1 Cup kitchen scraps

Put 1 cup of any brand of dry dog food into a bowl and add ½ cup warm water. Let stand until water is absorbed. Add kitchen scraps and rendered suet. Mix and spoon into muffin cups. Refrigerate to cool and harden. Toss several "muffins" on the ground at secondary feeder.

The Brown Thrasher, with its long tail, reddish-brown upper parts, and heavily streaked under-parts, is a shy bird. When attracted to your feeding station, Brown Thrashers will prefer your ground feeders.

THRASHER TREATS

½ Cup rendered suet
1 Cup bread crumbs
½ Cup raisins

½ Orange, cut into pieces
White proso millet

Put bread crumbs into a bowl and add raisins, orange pieces and millet. Pour rendered suet over mixture. Refrigerate to harden. Cut into pieces and serve at ground feeder.

The Hermit Thrush is brownish
gray with a rusty tail
and spotted breast.
Although shy, these birds
do like to nest in our
gardens and will
come to a ground feeder.

THRUSH TRIFLE

2	Cups rendered suet	4	Tbs. chopped prunes
1	slice white bread, quartered	4	Tbs. raisins
		4	Tbs. currants
		2	Tsp. grape jelly

Into each of 4 custard cups, put 1 bread square. Add 1 tablespoon each of chopped raisins, currants and prunes. Put ½ teaspoon grape jelly over chopped fruit and fill each cup with rendered suet. Allow to harden in refrigerator. Turn out onto low feeder table or ground feeder.

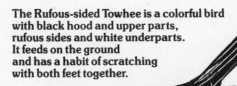

The Rufous-sided Towhee is a colorful bird
with black hood and upper parts,
rufous sides and white underparts.
It feeds on the ground
and has a habit of scratching
with both feet together.

TOWHEE TOAST

1   Cup rendered suet
2   Slices bread, toasted
Canary seed

Pour the rendered suet into a pieplate. Dip
each slice of toast into the suet and sprinkle
with canary seed. Allow to harden in refrigerator, cut into pieces and serve at ground
feeder.

THE WATERING HOLE

Provide your guests with a place to drink and bathe — it can be as simple or as elegant as you wish. We've all seen birds drinking and bathing in a puddle. Try to duplicate this scene when setting up your watering hole.

There are three important facts to remember. Birds are afraid of bathing in water that is too deep, so the water in your birdbaths should be an inch to an inch and a half at the most.

The nearest tree, shrub or fence should be three to four feet from the bath, as anything closer will provide cover for a lurking cat, and wet feathers can make a bird too heavy to fly a long distance.

Last, but not least, we all prefer to drink and bathe in clean, fresh water. Scrub your bird baths every second day and fill with cool fresh water.

In order to keep the water from freezing during the winter, you must use an immersion water heater, sold in garden and hardware centers.

MAINTAINING THE FEEDING STATION

The key to a healthy bird population at your feeder is the maintenance of your feeding stations. Keep your seed dispensers stocked with quality seed and keep them clean. After a rain, they become clogged with wet, spoiled grains. Empty the seed dispensers, wash with a mild detergent, and dry thoroughly with paper towels. Ground feeders should not be set up directly under seed dispensers, as bird droppings will contaminate the contents. Add clean sand or fine gravel periodically. Rake up and dispose of seed hulls in the area. Suet can turn rancid quickly, so check your suet containers during an early or late winter thaw. With your stations well-maintained, you are assured of a successful bird feeding program.

Canada $7.95

50595

9 780385 265010

N 0-385-26501-8>>595